Social Skills Activities

for Today's Kids

AGES

4–5

I0869518

Name:

Note to Parents

The activities in this book are designed to help your child think about social skills and how they can be used in everyday life at the park, at school, or at a store, for example. Learning social skills will be an important part of your child having friendships and other meaningful relationships, as well as positive interactions with his or her peers.

Provide support as your child does the activities. Read the directions aloud and complete the activities together, discussing your child's feelings and thoughts. Answer any questions your child has. Learning social skills can be challenging, so being patient and providing support as your child learns how to apply what he or she has learned to relationships and social situations is an important part of your child's experience.

Editorial Development: Tiffany Hailey
Teera Robinson
Lisa Vitarisi Mathews
Copy Editing: Laurie Westrich
Art Direction: Yuki Meyer
Cover Illustration: Dana Regan
Illustration: Mary Rojas
Design/Production: Jessica Onken

EVAN-MOOR Educational Publishers

EMC 3117

Congratulations on your purchase of some of the finest teaching materials in the world.

Evan-Moor Corporation
phone 1-800-777-4362, fax 1-800-777-4332.

10 Harris Court, Suite C-3, Monterey, CA 93940-5773. Printed in China.

CPSIA: Asia Pacific Offset Ltd, Kowloon, Hong Kong, China [11/2024]

002

CONTENTS

Making Friends

What Is a Friend? 8

What Friends Do 8
Friends Play 9
We Like the Same Things 10
Different and the Same 11
Friendship Painting 12
Color Mixing Guide 13
Friends Share 14
Sharing Is Caring 15
Friends Help 16
I Can Help 17
Friends Are Kind 18
Feeling Good 19
Nice Words 20
My Friend 23
Robot Friend 24

Making Friends 27

Find Friends 27
Where to Meet Friends 28
Friends at the Park 29
Say Hello to My Friend 30
A New Friend 33
Play with Me 34
Show How You Feel 37
Gingerbread Puppets 38
Gingerbread Puppet Words 41

Being a Good Friend 42

Good Friend Chart 42
Friendship Soup 43
Friends Take Turns 44
Use Your Words 45
Words That Make You Happy 46
When Friends Are Sad 47
Even When I'm Mad 48
Friends Puzzle 49
I Am a Good Friend 52
Fun with Friends 53
Good Friend Mobile 54

Contents continue on the next page.

Being at School

In the Classroom 60

At School 60
New Friends at School 61
Classroom Fun 62
We Can Be Different 63
School Friends Hat 64
Different Is Beautiful 67
Things I Can Do at School 68
Listening with My Body 69
Soft Voices 70
Your Turn to Talk 71
Clean Hands 72
My Things at School 73
I Can Use My Words 74
When I'm Mad or Sad 75
Thank a Classmate 76

Time to Eat 79

Things I Can Do When I Eat 79
Good Choices at the Table 80
Words I Can Say at Lunch 81
I Am Done 82
Eating with Someone New 83

Quiet Time 84

Resting Hand 84
Quiet Time Coloring 85
Quiet Art Shapes 86

On the Playground 89

On the Playground 89
Kindness on the Playground 90
Wait Your Turn 91
Safe on the Playground 92
Ask to Play 95
Friends on the Playground 96
Playing with Friends 99
Play by Myself 100
Not That Game 103
Line Up Hokey Pokey 104

Contents continue on the next page.

Going Places

Quiet Voice, Loud Voice 108

Going Places with My Family 108

I Speak Quietly 109

I Speak Loudly 110

Talking to People 111

I Say Hello 111

Hello, Neighborhood! 112

Using Kind Words 113

People's Pets 114

Making Good Choices 115

Healthy Choices 115

Eating at a Restaurant 116

Going to the Store 119

I Make Good Choices 120

Handbook 121

Making Friends

Making friends is fun.
Being a friend and having a friend is fun.
There are things to think about when you are a friend.

- ☆ What friends do
- ☆ How friends play
- ☆ How friends talk to each other

What Is a Friend?
Page 8

Making Friends
Page 27

Being a Good Friend
Page 42

What Friends Do

Look at the pictures.
Trace the words that tell what friends do.

Friends play.

Friends share.

Friends help.

Friends are kind.

Friends Play

Friends like to do things together.

Color the pictures that show what you like to do with a friend.

paint

dance

read

play

We Like the Same Things

Some friends like the same things.

Draw a line to match the kids that are doing the same things.

What Is a Friend?

Different and the Same

People may look different from you,
but in many ways you are the same.
Friends can be different.

Draw a picture of your face.
Then draw a picture of your friend's face.

me	my friend

Circle the body parts you and your friend both have.

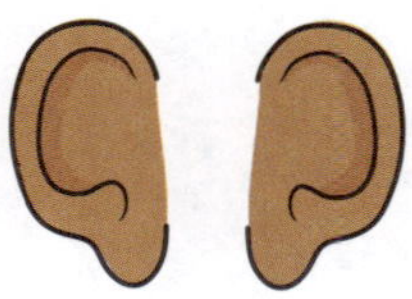

ears

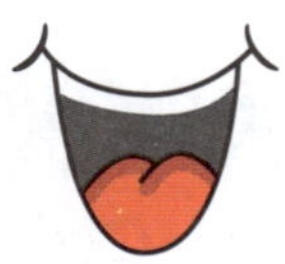

mouth

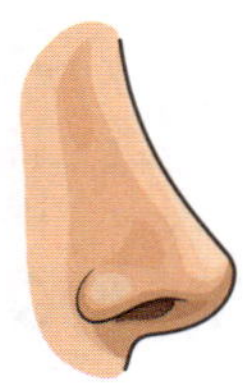

nose

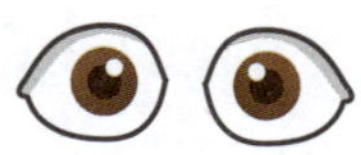

eyes

Circle **yes** or **no** to answer the questions.

Do you look the same?	yes	no
Can friends be different?	yes	no

Friendship Painting

Mixing two different colors together can make something beautiful, just like a friendship.

Make a painting with your friend.

What You Need

- red, yellow, and blue paint
- page 13
- large white paper or poster board
- paper plates

What You Do

1. Put one color of paint on a paper plate. Do this for each color.
2. Look at the Color Mixing Guide on page 13.
3. Put one of your hands in one color and make a handprint on the white paper. Have your friend do the same with a different color.
4. Next, rub your painted hand with your friend's hand to mix the two colors. Then make handprints on the white paper.
5. Look at the the beautiful new color you made!

Color Mixing Guide

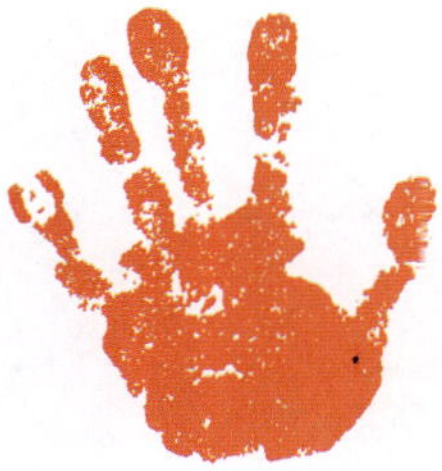 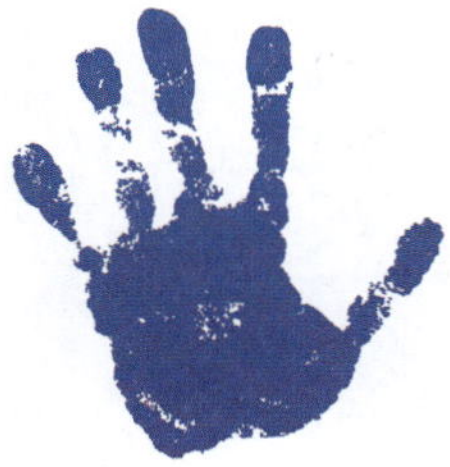 

red + blue = purple

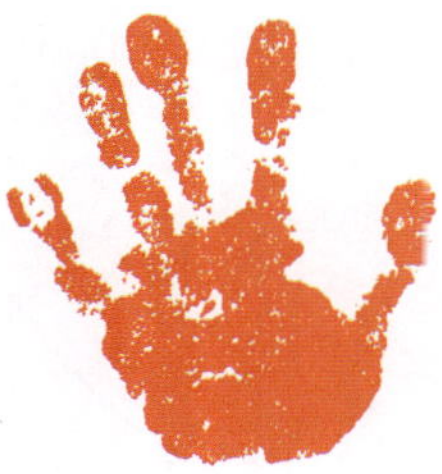  

red + yellow = orange

blue + yellow = green

Friends Share

A friend shares.

The friends like to eat cookies.
Share the cookies by drawing one cookie on each plate.

Sharing Is Caring

Cut out the toys.
Glue a toy next to each friend to share.

Friends Help

A friend helps.

Oh no! Max lost all his marbles!
Draw a line through the maze
to help Max find his marbles.

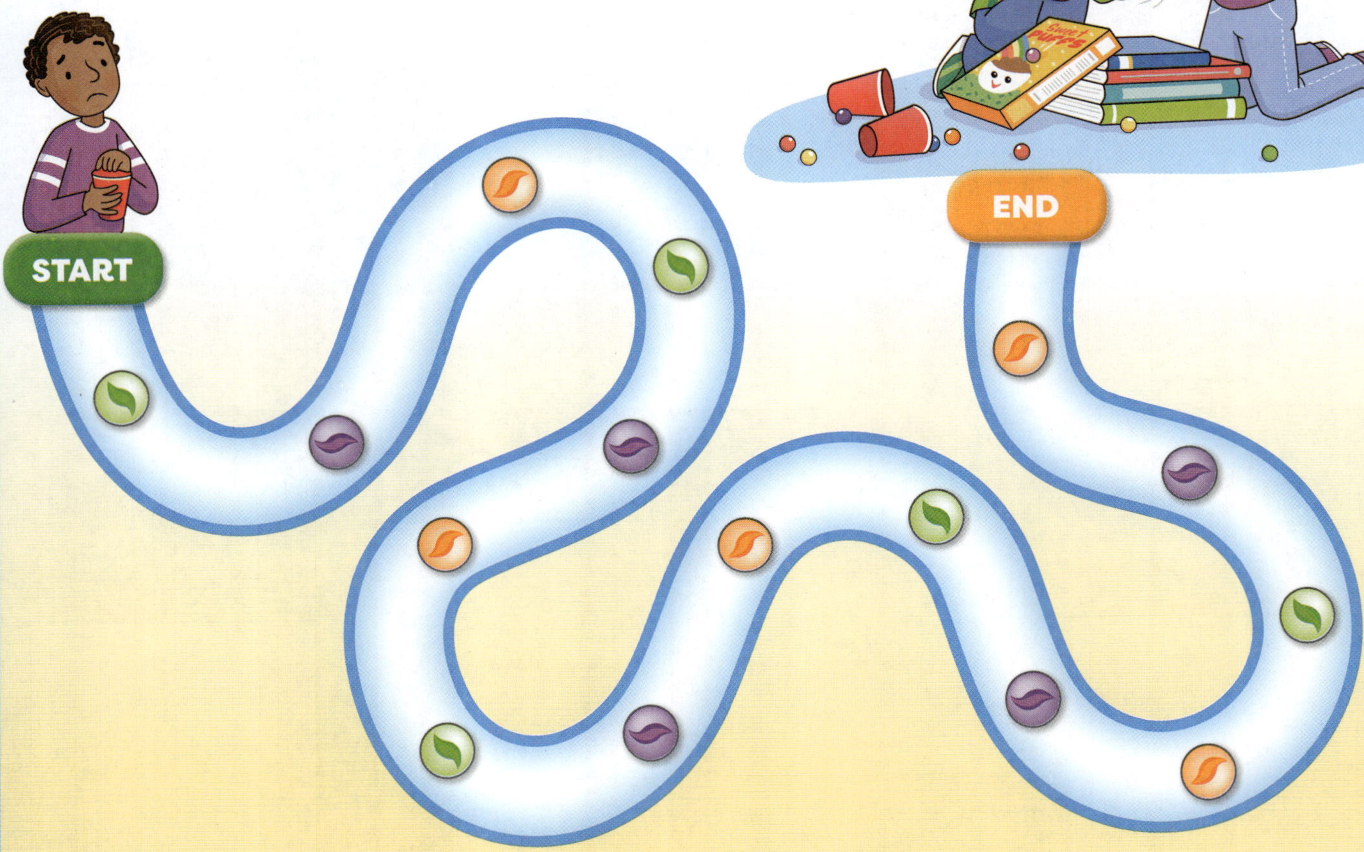

I Can Help

Help the boy paint the pots.
Finish the pattern.
Color the pots.

Friends Are Kind

Friends are kind to each other.
Friends play nicely together.

Color 🙂 if the kids are being kind.

Color 🙁 if the kids are not being kind.

Feeling Good

Friends make you smile. Friends make you feel special. Having friends feels good.

Draw 2 more ☺.
Color all of them.
Then write how many in all.

Draw 3 more ★.
Color all of them.
Then write how many in all.

Draw 1 more ♥.
Color all of them.
Then write how many in all.

Nice Words

A friend says nice words.

Cut out the puzzle pieces on page 21.
Glue the puzzle piece to tell what each friend can say.

glue

glue

glue

thank you

please

excuse me

My Friend

Write your friend's name.
Then draw pictures.

My friend's name is ______________________________ .
This is what my friend looks like.

My favorite thing to do with my friend

What Is a Friend?

Robot Friend

Friends work together. Friends listen to each other.

You and a friend can work together to build a robot.

What You Need

- page 25
- construction paper
- markers
- scissors
- glue

What You Do

1. Cut out the shapes on page 25.
2. Talk with your friend about how you want the robot to look. Listen to what your friend says. Say how you feel, too.
3. Take turns gluing the shapes on construction paper to make a robot.
4. If you'd like, use markers to draw more shapes.
5. Give your friend a high five when you're done!

Find Friends

Trace the word.
Then find the letters in the picture. Circle them.

friends

Where to Meet Friends

Making Friends

You can meet new friends at different places in your town.

Trace the lines to show where you can meet new friends.

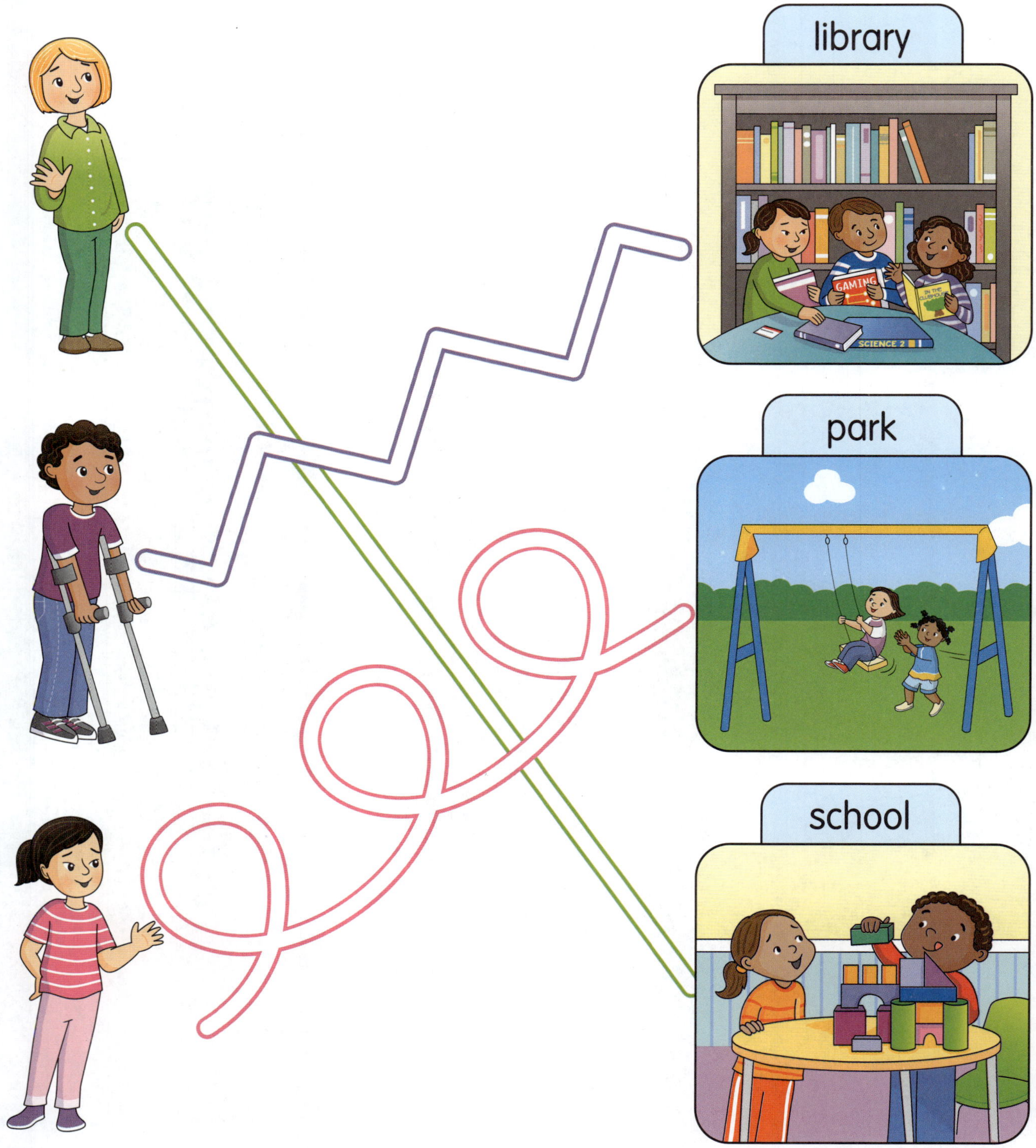

Friends at the Park

Look at the picture.
Count and write how many friends are playing at the park.

I see ________ friends.

Say Hello to My Friend

You can make friends by saying "Hello."
There are many ways to say hello.

Cut out the pictures on page 31.
Glue ways you like to say hello on the yellow boxes.
Glue ways you want to try to say hello on the red boxes.

Ways I like to say hello	Ways to say hello that I want to try
glue	glue
glue	glue
glue	glue

A New Friend

If you see someone playing alone, you can ask him or her to play with you.

Color the boxes to get to the friend.

Follow the pattern ● ♥ ★.

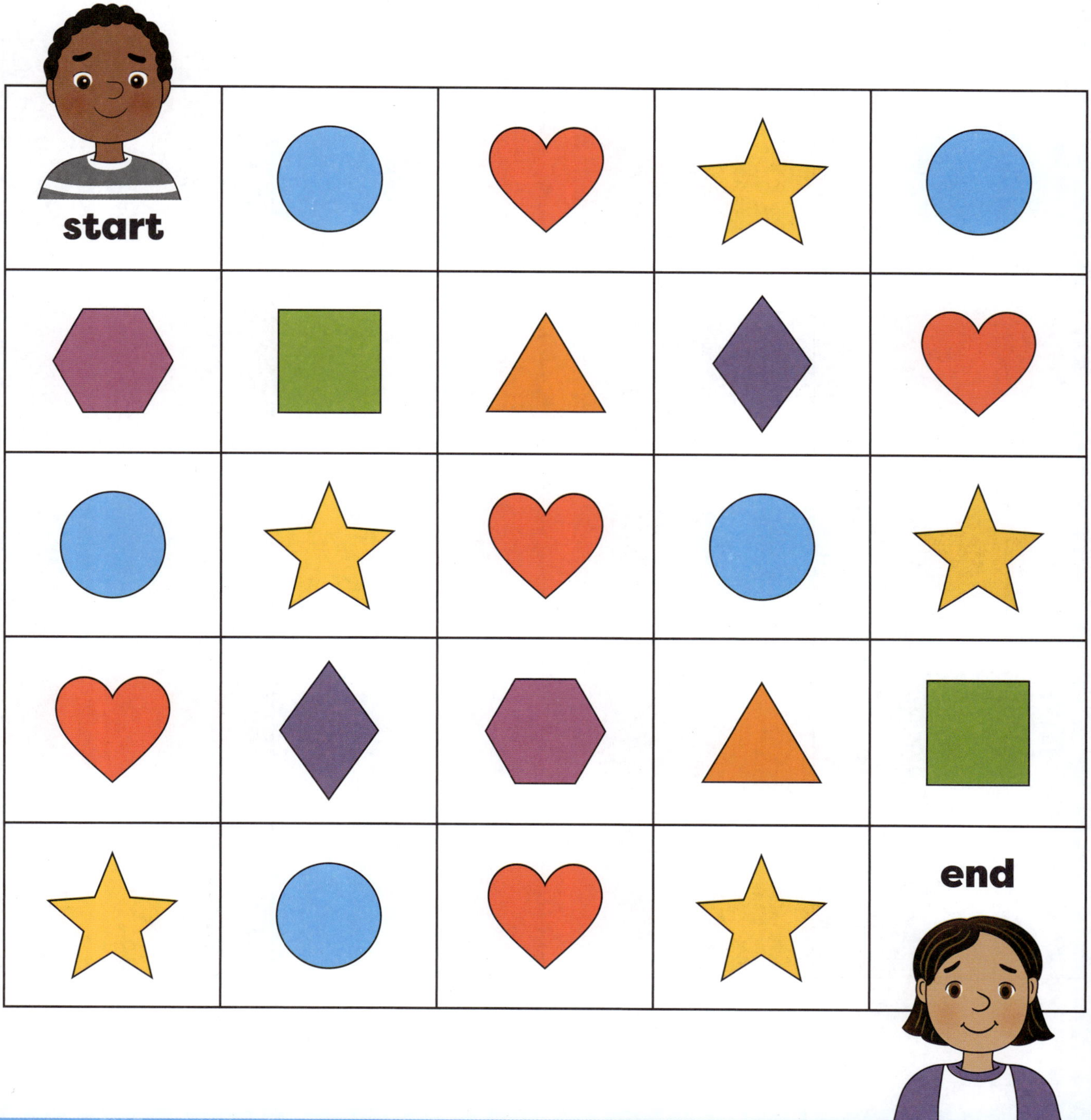

Play with Me

Cut out the pieces on page 35.
Glue them below to see how you can ask a friend to play.

glue	glue	glue	glue

nt to
Do y
play?
ou wa

Show How You Feel

Your face can show how you feel.

Look at each face.
Trace the word that tells how each face feels.

mad

happy

sad

Circle the kids that look like they want to play.

Making Friends

Gingerbread Puppets

You can practice talking to people.
You can practice making new friends.

Make puppets to practice what to say when making new friends.

What You Need

- pages 39 and 41
- crayons or markers
- scissors
- two craft sticks or straws
- glue or tape

What You Do

1. Color the gingerbread people on page 39. Then cut them out.
2. Glue or tape a craft stick or straw to the back of each puppet.
3. Use the puppets to practice what to say to new friends. Finish the sentence on page 41 for words the puppets can say.

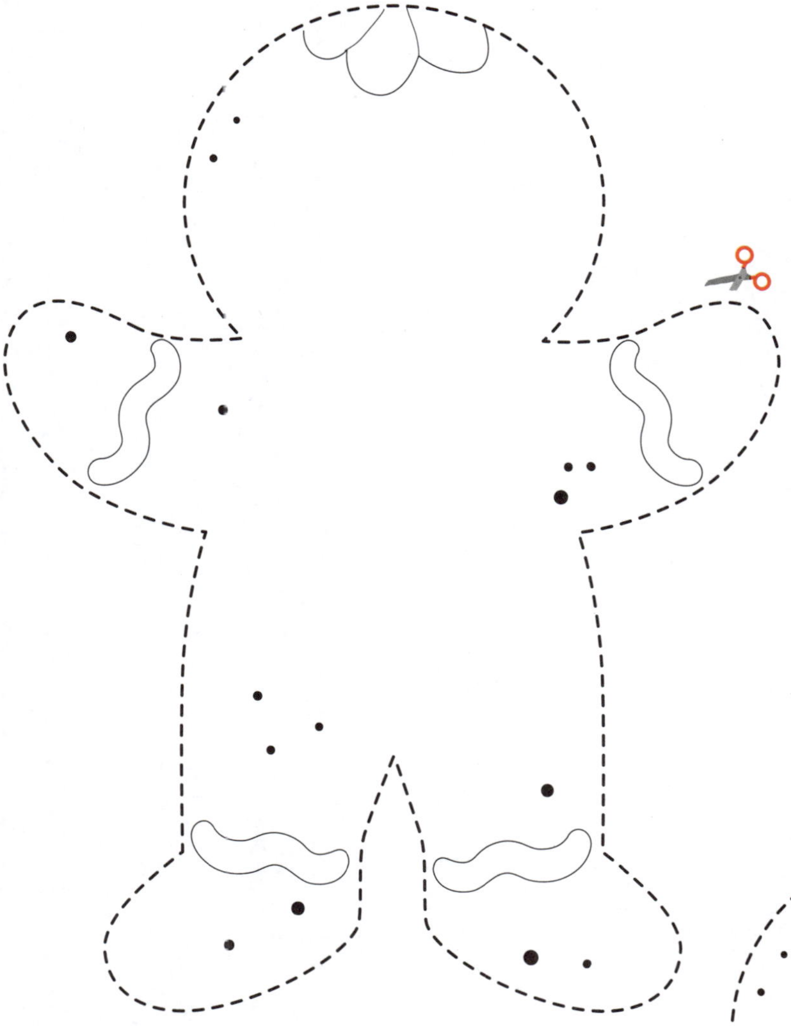

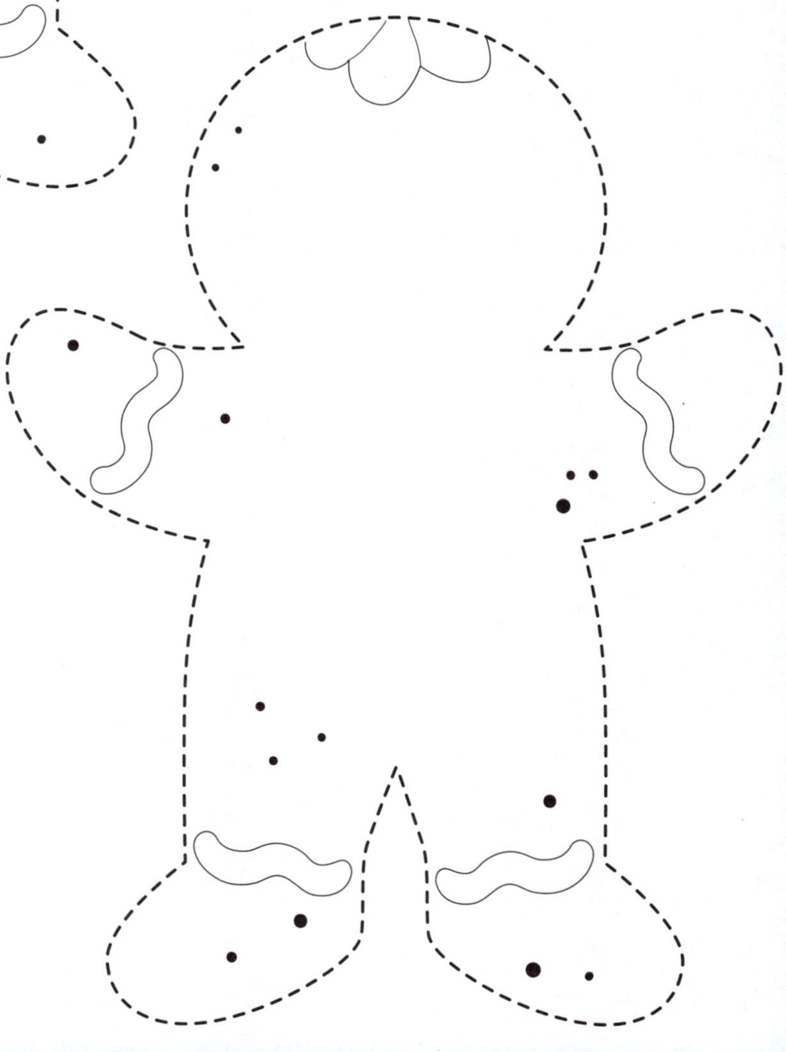

Gingerbread Puppet Words

You can use the puppets you made to practice talking to people and making new friends.

You can use the words below or your own words.

Hello!

My name is ______________________________.

What is your name?

Do you want to play?

Being a Good Friend

Good Friend Chart

Look at the pictures and read the words in each square.
They tell ways to be a good friend.
Pick one to do. After you do it, put an **X** on the box.

Hug a friend.

Share a toy.

Say hello.

Let a friend choose what to play.

Say kind words.

Listen to a friend.

Draw a picture for a friend.

Make a friend laugh.

Help a friend.

Being a Good Friend

Friendship Soup

Cut out the vegetables.
Glue them on the pot to tell what ingredients make a good friend.

 **helps**	 **is kind**	 **listens**

Friends Take Turns

Gina wants to swing,
but Bailey sat down first.
What should Gina do?

Color the circle below the picture that shows what you think Gina should do.

○ wait for her turn

○ take the swing from Bailey

Being a Good Friend

Use Your Words

Friends use words to tell you how they feel.
It is important to listen to the words your friends say.

Jason wants to play with a friend.
Draw a line to the friend who says **yes**.

no

Do you want to play?

yes

Words That Make You Happy

The words you say can help a friend feel happy.

Read the sentences. Trace the words.

You are kind.

You are funny.

You make me happy.

When Friends Are Sad

You can say words that help friends feel better when they are sad or mad.

Read the sentences. Trace the words.

I am sorry.

Are you okay?

I will help you.

Being a Good Friend

Even When I'm Mad

Sometimes friends get mad at each other.
But you can make a good choice even when you feel mad.

Luke is mad.
He wants to play with the toy car.
But Jessie is playing with it.

Color the circle below the picture that shows Luke making a good choice.

Friends Puzzle

Friends fit together like a puzzle piece.

Cut out the puzzle pieces below.
Glue them on page 51.

Friends Puzzle

glue	glue	glue
glue	glue	glue
glue	glue	glue

I Am a Good Friend

Read the sentence.
Draw a picture to show how you are a good friend.

I play with my friends.

I share with my friends.

I help my friends.

I am kind.

Being a Good Friend

Fun with Friends

Color the picture.

Good Friend Mobile

Make a mobile to show everyone why you are a good friend.

What You Need

- pages 55–58
- crayons or markers
- scissors
- glue
- hole punch
- string

What You Do

1. Cut out the mobile on page 55. Use a hole punch to make two holes at the top of the page and three holes at the bottom of the page. Then glue the ends of the page together to make a tube shape.
2. Cut out the shapes on page 57. Use a hole punch to make a hole at the top of each shape.
3. Pull a piece of string through one of the holes at the bottom of the tube and the top of one shape. Tie the string in a knot. Do this for all of the shapes.
4. Last, pull a piece of string through the holes on the top of the tube, tie it in a knot, and hang your mobile in your bedroom!

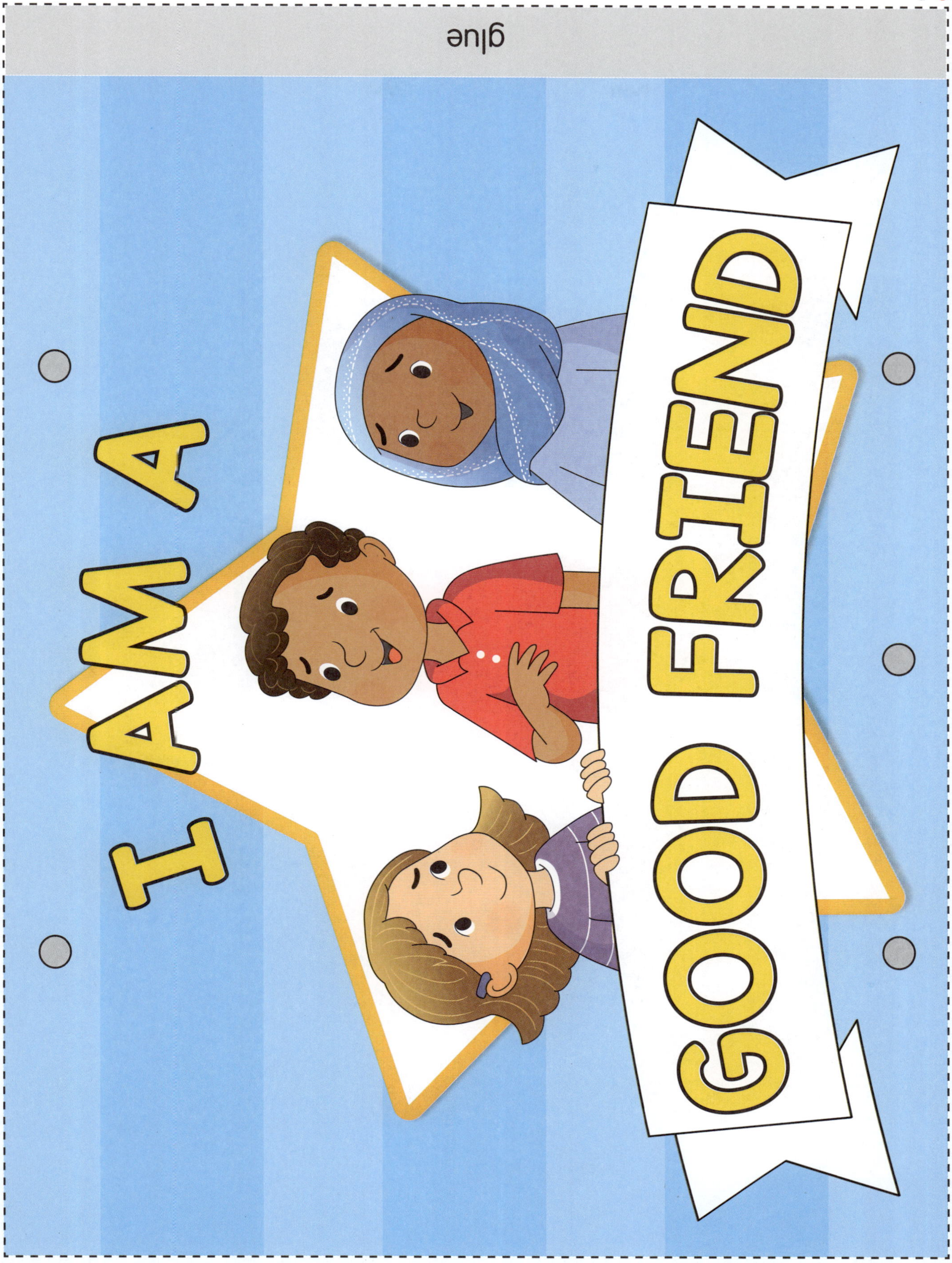
glue
I AM A
GOOD FRIEND

fun

kind

helpful

kind

fun

helpful

Being at School

Being at school is fun.
There are things to think about when you are at school.

- ☆ What you do at school
- ☆ How you act at school
- ☆ How you eat at school
- ☆ How you play at school

In the Classroom
Page 60

Time to Eat
Page 79

Quiet Time
Page 84

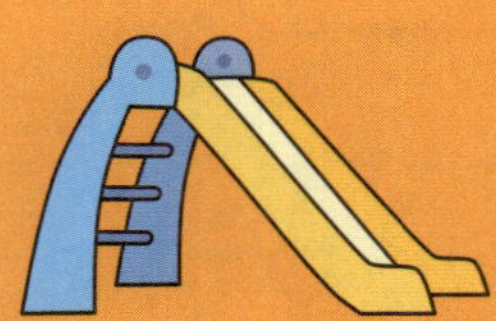

On the Playground
Page 89

At School

There are many things to do at school.

Look at the pictures of things you can do at school.
Color the circles to show the things you like to do.

New Friends at School

You can meet new friends at school.

Trace the lines to help each child make a friend at school.

Classroom Fun

In the Classroom

There are many fun things you can do with friends in the classroom.

Look at the pictures of children having fun in the classroom. Color the circles to show the things you like to do.

We Can Be Different

In the Classroom

Every child is different.
You can be friends with children who are different from you.

Draw pictures to tell about you and one of your friends.

Me	My Friend
my favorite food	my friend's favorite food
my favorite animal	my friend's favorite animal
this is what I like to do	this is what my friend likes to do

In the Classroom

School Friends Hat

Friends in your class help make school fun.
Make a hat that shows all your new friends from school.

What You Need

- friends hat cutout on page 65
- scissors
- glue or tape
- crayons or markers

What You Do

1. Have a grown-up cut out the friends hat on page 65.
2. Use crayons or markers to draw your friends from your class on the people shapes.
3. Glue or tape the ends of the hat together.
4. Wear your hat to show your family all your new friends from school.

I like my school friends!
glue
glue

Different Is Beautiful

In the Classroom

Read the poem. Then color the picture.

My friends are not the same, and that is okay.

We are all beautiful in our own way.

Like a rainbow, we come in many colors.

How great it is to be different from each other.

Things I Can Do at School

You can do things at school that help you and your classmates learn and stay safe.

Read the sentence. Then color the picture.

I can listen to the teacher.

I can raise my hand and wait for my turn to talk.

I can use my hands in kind ways.

I can keep the classroom clean.

Listening with My Body

Cut and glue to show how you can listen in the classroom.

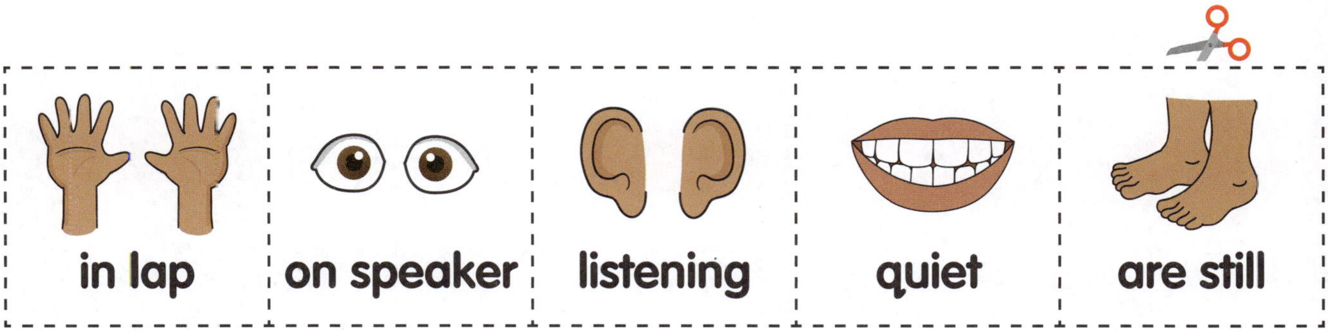

Soft Voices

Look at the pictures. When do you need to use a soft voice? Color the circle.

○

○

○

○

Your Turn to Talk

When you want to talk in the classroom, raise your hand. Wait for the teacher to say your name. Then you can talk.

Cut and glue the numbers in order **1**, **2**, **3** to show what to do when you want to talk in the classroom.

glue

I raise my hand.

glue

I wait for the teacher to say my name.

glue

Then I talk.

1	2	3

Clean Hands

You can help keep your classroom clean by washing your hands.

Write **1**, **2**, **3**, **4** in the boxes to show how to wash your hands.

☐ 

Wet your hands and get soap.

☐ 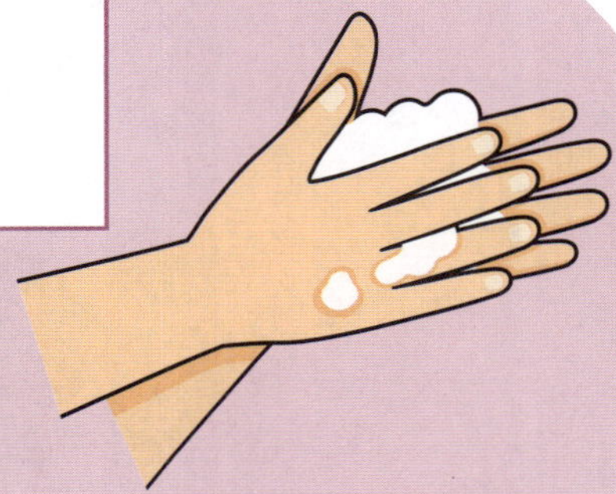

Rub your hands together.

☐ 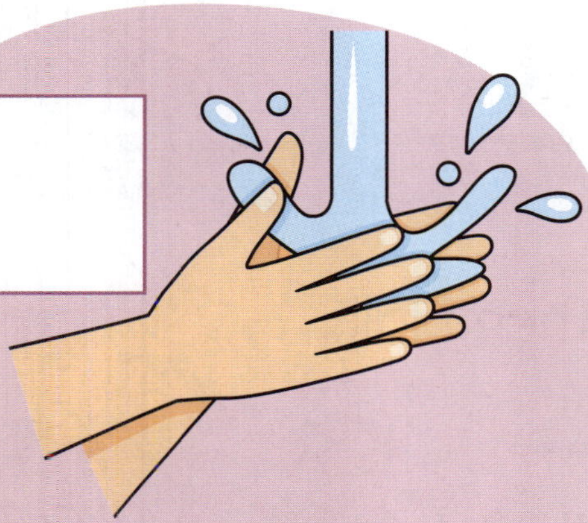

Rinse your hands with water.

☐ 

Dry your hands.

My Things at School

You can bring things to school, like a jacket or a lunchbox. You can bring things to school that will help you learn, like paper and a pencil.

Draw a line to the backpack to show what things you would bring to school.

toy train

crayons

book

cat

pencil

scissors

Color the face to show how you would feel if someone took things from your backpack.

 happy

 mad

 sad

I Can Use My Words

In the Classroom

Sometimes kids in your class will do things you do not like. You can say words to tell them how you feel.

Look at the pictures. Trace the words.

No!

Stop!

I do not like that.

When I'm Mad or Sad

Sometimes things happen at school that make you feel mad or sad. You can do things to feel better.

Read. Then color the pictures that show what you can do to feel better.

count to 10

talk to a friend

talk to your teacher

have some quiet time

Thank a Classmate

You can say thank you when a child in your class does something for you.

Give children in your class a thank-you shape for being a great classmate.

What You Need

- cutouts on page 77
- crayons or markers
- scissors

What You Do

1. Color the shapes on page 77. Make sure to color around the words so your friends can still read them.
2. Think about whom you want to give a thank-you shape to.
3. Write a classmate's name on the back of each shape.
4. Then give it to your classmate to tell him or her how you feel.

Thank you for being kind.

Thank you for helping me.

Thank you for playing with me.

Thank you for making me laugh.

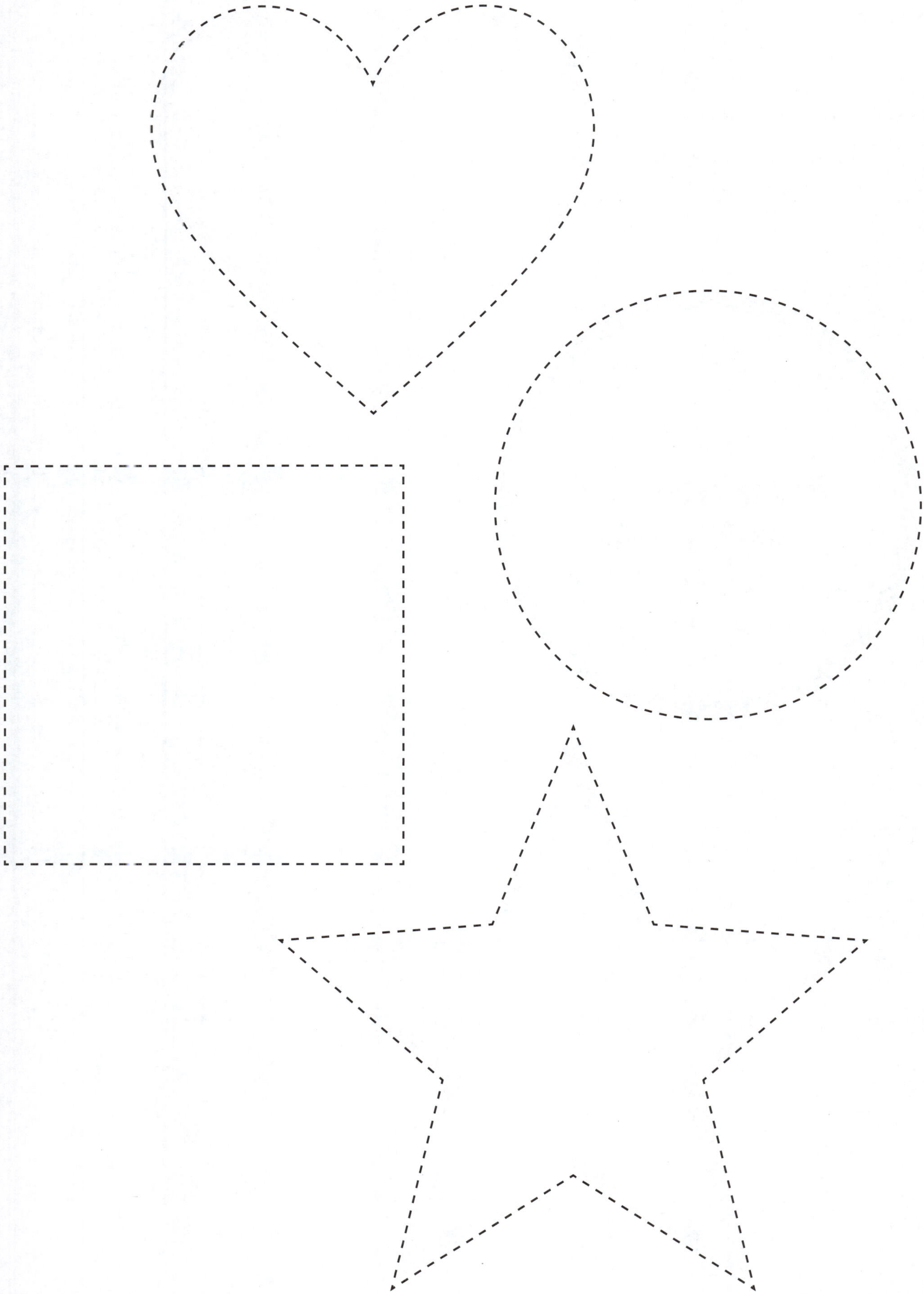

Things I Can Do When I Eat

There are things you can do when you eat with others at school.

Look at the pictures that show kids eating nicely at school. Draw a ☺ in each box to tell them good job!

I can sit in a chair and not get up until I finish eating.

I can talk when my mouth is not filled with food.

I can use a napkin.

I can throw my trash in the garbage.

Good Choices at the Table

Look at the pictures.

Color 👍 if the kids are making good choices.

Color 👎 if the kids are not making good choices.

Words I Can Say at Lunch

There are words you can say when you eat.
You can use your hands to talk, too.

Draw a line to match the words to the picture.

More, please!

Thank you!

All done!

Thank you!

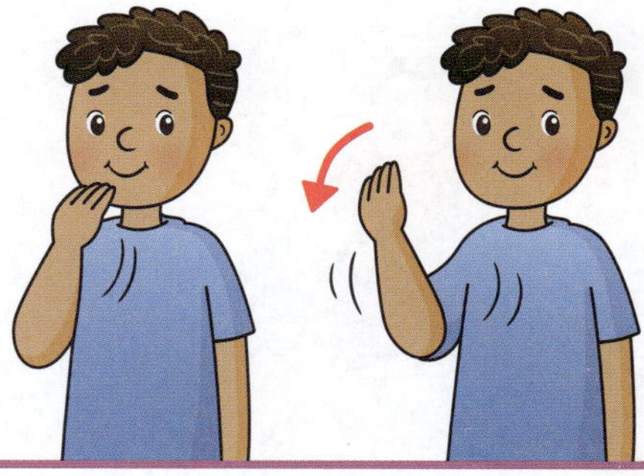

All done!

More, please!

I Am Done

When you are done eating, you can clean up.
You can wipe your face with a napkin.
You can throw away your trash.
You can wash your hands, too.

All the kids are done eating.
Help them get what they need.
Trace the lines.

Eating with Someone New

You can ask someone new to eat with you.

Cut out the shapes below.
Glue them to see how you can ask someone to eat with you.
Then color the picture.

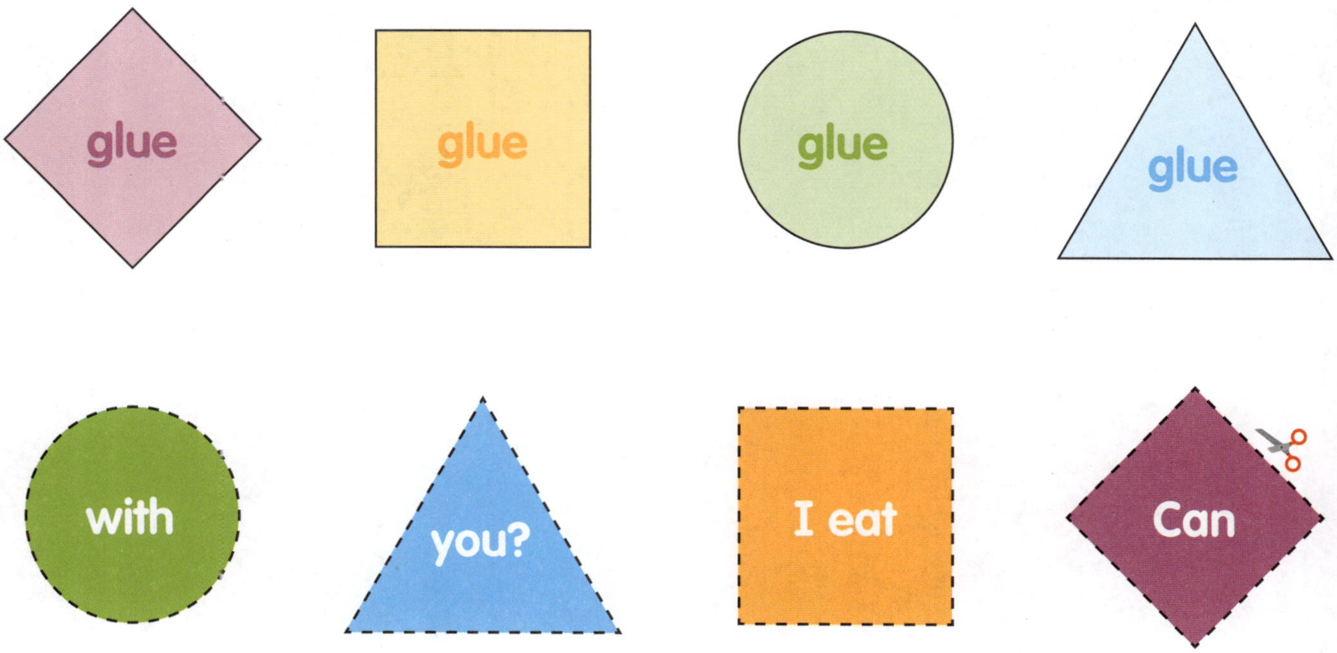

Quiet Time

Resting Hand

Sometimes it can be hard to rest. You can breathe in and out slowly to help your mind and body rest.

Trace the hand.
Slowly breathe in and out as you trace each finger.

Quiet Time Coloring

Sometimes it is nice to sit in a quiet space and color.
Having quiet time can make you feel good.

Color the picture in a quiet space.
Think about how you feel as you color.

Quiet Art Shapes

You can make an art project to quiet your mind and body.

Quiet Art Shapes

What You Need

- Quiet Art Shapes on page 87
- pipe cleaners
- optional: glue

What You Do

1. Remove page 87 from the book. Put it on a table.
2. Breathe in and out slowly as you bend pipe cleaners to make the shapes on the page.
3. If you'd like to, use glue to stick your shapes to the page.
4. When quiet time is over, show a friend what you made.

Quiet Art Shapes

On the Playground

You can do things on the playground that help you and other kids have fun and stay safe.

Read the sentence. Then color the ☆ if you think you can do these things on the playground.

I can share and take turns.

I can slide down feet first and swing on my bottom.

I can clean up my toys.

I can line up nicely when the bell rings.

Kindness on the Playground

It is important to be kind when you play.

Color the pictures that show ways to be kind.

It's your turn now.

Helping is kind.

Using gentle hands is kind.

Wait Your Turn

On the Playground

Waiting for your turn to talk or play a game can be hard.
But you can do it!

Trace the numbers **1**, **2**, and **3** to show what to do when you have to wait for your turn.

Step 1

stop

Step 2

Take a deep breath.

Step 3

Wait for your turn.

Safe on the Playground

Oh no, the kids are not playing safely! You can help. Cut out the pictures on page 93. Glue them on top of the pictures below to show the kids playing safely.

I sit on the swing.

I slide on my bottom.

I throw balls.

I use my hands in kind ways.

Ask to Play

On the Playground

You can ask a friend to play.
Say hello, then ask him or her to play.

Circle how you like to say hello.

fist bump

smile and wave

say hello

Circle one way you would like to ask someone to play with you.

Do you want to play with me?

Can I play, too?

Friends on the Playground

Cut out the pieces on page 97.
Glue them below to see how you can ask a friend to play.

glue	glue	glue	glue

I play | you? | with | Can

Playing with Friends

Trace the words to write a sentence that tells about what you can do with friends on the playground.

We can run.

We can jump.

We can play.

Play by Myself

On the Playground

Sometimes you may not want to play with other people. You can tell a friend in a nice way that you want to play by yourself.

Look at the pictures. Cut out the puzzle pieces on page 101. Glue them to finish the puzzles.

Do you want to play with me?

glue

Can I play with you?

glue

Will you play with me?

glue

No, thank you.

Maybe next time.

Sorry, I want to play by myself.

Not That Game

Sometimes a friend may not want to play the same thing as you do, and that is okay. You can make another choice, and so can your friend.

Color the things you can do if a friend does not want to play the same thing as you do.

make a mean face

ask why

play with another friend

yell at your friend

Line Up Hokey Pokey

Sing the song about lining up to the tune of the "Hokey Pokey" song.

Find the picture that matches the song. Then glue it below the song.

I listen with my ears,
I look straight with my eyes,
I have a quiet mouth,
And keep my hands to my side,
I use my walking feet,
And I don't turn around,
That's what it's all about!

glue

Going Places

Going places can be fun.
There are things to think about when you go places.

- ☆ How to act
- ☆ How to say hello to people
- ☆ How to make healthy and safe choices

Quiet Voice, Loud Voice — Page 108

Talking to People — Page 111

Making Good Choices — Page 115

Quiet Voice, Loud Voice

Going Places with My Family

There are many places you go with your family.

Look at the pictures. Circle the places you have been.

I Speak Quietly

There are places you use a quiet voice.

Color the pictures of places you use a quiet voice.

You use a quiet voice at a library.

You use a quiet voice at a restaurant.

You use a quiet voice at a store.

I Speak Loudly

There are places you can use a loud voice.

Color the pictures of places you can use a loud voice.

You can use a loud voice at the park.

You can use a loud voice at a sports game.

Draw one more place you can use a loud voice.

I Say Hello

You can say **hello** to people when you go places.

Trace the lines to help the people say hello.

Hello, Neighborhood!

You can say **hello** to people in your neighborhood.

Draw a line to help the family get home.
Trace the different ways to say hi to the people along the way.

Using Kind Words

When you go places and talk to people, you can use kind words.

Look at the pictures. Then trace the words.

thank you

excuse me

please

People's Pets

You see pets when you go places.
If you want to touch a pet or give it a treat,
you and your parent must talk to the pet's owner first.

Each of these kids asked before they touched or fed the pet.

Can I pet your cat?

Can I hold your mouse?

May I give your dog a treat?

Color the pets you would like to play with.

Healthy Choices

Making Good Choices

You can make choices that keep you and other people healthy.

Color 😊 or ☹️ to show if the kids are making healthy choices.

Wash your hands.

Pick your nose.

Use a tissue.

Cover your cough and sneeze.

Making Good Choices

Eating at a Restaurant

You can make choices that show respect and kindness when you eat in restaurants.

Read the sentences. Then cut out the pictures on page 117 and glue them to match the sentences.

glue

I stay in my seat at the table.

glue

I chew with my mouth closed.

glue

I use a napkin.

glue

I say kind words like "please" and "thank you."

Thank you!
Menu

7

Going to the Store

Making Good Choices

You can make choices that keep yourself and others safe when you are in a store.

Which kids are making good choices?
Draw a line from the picture to the words.

I do not run in the store.

I keep my hands to myself.

I use a cart safely.

Color the picture.

Note: Cut apart the pages. Put them in order. Staple them together.

staple

My Social Skills Handbook

staple

CONTENTS

Making Friends

Page 2

Being at School

Page 6

Going Places

Page 10

You are learning about social skills. Good for you!

Learning about social skills can help you make friends. It can also help you think about what to do and how to act when you go to school. Learning about social skills can help you feel okay when you go to places like restaurants and stores.

You can look at this handbook to remind you of what you learned about social skills.

How Friends Act

Friends do kind things for each other.

Friends play nicely.

Friends share.

Friends help.

What Friends Do

There are many things friends like to do together.

Friends paint.

Friends dance.

Friends play.

How Friends Talk

Friends talk to each other nicely.

thank you

please

sorry

Where Friends Meet

You can meet a new friend in many places.

at the park

at school

at a library

What You Do at School

There are many things you do at school.

You learn.

You eat.

You make friends.

How You Act at School

You do things to follow the rules and be kind at school.

You listen.

You help.

You follow the rules.

What You Can Do When You Are Mad or Sad

You can do these things when you feel mad or sad at school.

Count to ten.

Talk to a teacher.

Have quiet time.

What You Do When You Eat at School

You can do these things when you eat with others at school.

Use a napkin.

Put my trash in the garbage.

Talk before taking a bite of food.

Where You Speak Quietly

There are places you can use a quiet voice.

at a store

at a restaurant

at a library

How You Talk

You can use kind words when you go places.

thank you

excuse me

yes, please

How You Make Healthy Choices

You can make healthy choices when you go places.

Wash your hands.

Cover your cough and sneeze.

Use a tissue.

How You Stay Safe

You can make choices that keep you safe when you go places.

Use a cart safely.

Ask before you pet.

Walk in a store.